I Believe In Me!
How Little Ideas Become Big Dreams

Written by:
Dinah E. Corona
& Luisa F. Molano

Illustrated by:
Angie Alape

Halo
PUBLISHING
INTERNATIONAL

Halo Publishing International
7550 WIH-10 #800, PMB 2069,
San Antonio, TX 78229

First Edition, November 2023
ISBN: 978-1-63765-520-7
Library of Congress Control Number: 2023920135

Halo Publishing International is a self-publishing company that publishes adult fiction and non-fiction, children's literature, self-help, spiritual, and faith-based books. Do you have a book idea you would like us to consider publishing? Please visit www.halopublishing.com for more information.

Dreamers and doers of all ages,
this book is a magical wish for you.
Each day, may you wake up ready
to take another leap toward
the life and world about which you dream.

Thanks to you, the future shines with hope,
glistens with brightness,
and beams with beauty.

Keep dreaming, daring,
and always remember:
You are the magical hero of your own story!

Did you know you can make big things happen if you believe in yourself? This is the fun-tastic tale of Dinah, her Auntie Luisa, and how a teeny-weeny idea grew into a BIG thing.

On a fun vacation day, Dinah and Auntie Luisa were lost in the magical world created by books. Suddenly, Dinah said, "I love books! When I'm big, I'll write one!

Auntie Luisa, twinkling eyes full of mischief, replied, "Guess what? You don't have to wait till you're all grown up. We can start writing a book now!"

Dinah's eyes widened. "But isn't book writing a grown-up thing?"

"Dinah, remind me again. What are the three magical words that describe who you are?" asked Auntie Luisa.

"Smart, beautiful, and brave, Auntie," replied Dinah.

9

"That's right," said Auntie Luisa. "And since that's true, what do you think a brave little girl would do now?"

"I would believe in myself and my idea," replied Dinah.

How Dinah talks about herself matters, and so do her ideas.

Guess what? The same goes for you!

Ideas into Action

What are your three magic words?

 _____

 _____

 _____

What is your brilliant idea?

 _____

 _____

 _____

_____

Dinah and Auntie Luisa want every awesome reader of this book to know how vital it is to believe in yourself and your ideas.

They also want you to know that every idea in the world, big or small, happens ONE step at a time.

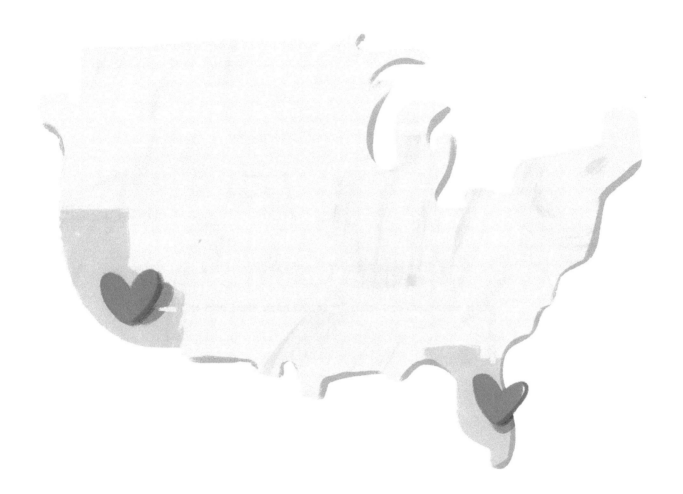

Auntie Luisa and Dinah live in different states, so they use FaceTime to chat and have weekly heartstorms.

what is a
heartstorm?

Everything in this book is a result of their heartstorms.

You know how brainstorming is using our heads to solve problems? Well, heartstorming is when two hearts join forces to create something really special!

As the weeks passed, the book began to come together!
One step at a time, they were doing it. Dinah and
Auntie Luisa were writing a book!

Big and brilliant ideas can feel like mountains
if we try to think of all the steps at once!

BELIEVE

20

But if we focus on the next small pebble right in front of us, even climbing the highest mountain can feel like a fun hike.

Ideas into action

The smallest step I can take with my brilliant idea is:

be brave ♡

When Dinah and Luisa started to work on the cover of their book, something big happened. Something really big.

Dinah didn't want her full name on the cover of the book. She only wanted her first name.

Auntie Luisa asked, "Dinah, why don't you want your beautiful last name on the book's cover?"

Dinah softly replied, "Some of the kids at school said Corona is a bad thing. They said Corona made lots of people sick, so my name is yucky."

"What do YOU think about your name, Dinah?" asked Auntie Luisa.

Dinah beamed. "I love it. It's the name of my family."

"Dinah, that sounds smart, beautiful, and brave. And guess what? 'Corona' means crown in Spanish.

"Next time, with the biggest smile, you can tell those kids your name is royal, and you proudly wear it!"

Auntie Luisa continued, "People often have opinions about others—their names, looks, beliefs, and other things.

"Remember, Dinah, you always have the choice to use words that help to lift others up, starting with the words you use about yourself!"

"You mean that I'm smart, beautiful, and brave?" Dinah asked.

"Exactly!" Auntie Luisa replied.

"Cool!" Dinah grinned.

Ideas into action

What do you love about yourself?

_____

_____

_____

_____

_____

32

With their book cover as bright as a rainbow, Dinah and Auntie Luisa were ready to send their book to the publisher to be printed!

When their book came back, holding it in their hands felt as if they were hugging a star.

They did it! They believed in themselves and their idea, and created a book together, one brave step at a time.

The book in your hands is proof that a tiny idea can become a big thing when you believe in yourself.

See you on the twinkling path of glitter and rainbows!

Acknowledgments

Writing a book truly takes a village. Tremendous thanks to...

Townsend, for being my number one fan and supporting my soul's fullest expression in every way. You are my favorite human on Earth—thanks for life-ing with me.

Cristina and Isaac, for being such conscious parents to Dinah (and Atticus) and raising such brave and bold little humans. You are an inextricable part of the magic that is in this book.

Jamie Rogers, for your support of my work in the world. I am deeply grateful. You allow me to spend more time in my zone of genius, dreaming, and scheming! You see me, and this book wouldn't be in the hands of others without your light. I love who you are.

Angie and Michelle, for being a vital part of this dream-made reality; I will always be grateful for that. Together, we have created more than a book; we've crafted an adventure that will hopefully inspire dreamers of all ages to believe in themselves, dream big, and take brave steps forward. I couldn't close out these acknowledgments without expressing my gratitude to you two.

Dinah and I share this accomplishment with all of you. Thank you for helping us make *I Believe in Me!* a reality.

About the Authors

Luisa F. Molano is a proud auntie to Dinah; her brother, Atticus; and their cousins Jorgie, Benji, Charlie, and Penelope Rose. She is the founder of Path to Purpose, a stirring speaker, author, and certified embodiment coach who's been empowering souls and success since 2017. Luisa works with individuals and groups, and does talks/workshops throughout her community. Luisa and Dinah are on a mission to impact one million lives with the message in *I Believe in Me!* She, along with her husband, Townsend Wardlaw, and their Morkie, Jax, call sunny St. Pete, Florida, home six months out of the year. The other six are spent working and traveling in various states and countries.

Meet Dinah E. Corona! She's not just any seven-year-old; she's a rising star at Las Lomas Elementary School in La Habra, California. Dinah is proud to be part of an extraordinary group called Las Lomas Entrepreneurs–Project Kids, where she and her classmates use unique ideas to improve their community. In 2023, she even learned how to code a robot with her friend! When she isn't busy with her innovative projects, you'll find her curled up with a good book, savoring rainbow sherbet, or munching popcorn while watching her favorite movies. But what Dinah loves most is art! And guess what? She's made her dream come true with this book, proving that dreams really can come true! A big shout-out goes to Mrs. Goodman, her supportive teacher who has been a big fan of Dinah's book-writing adventure.

And here's a message from Dinah just for you:
"No matter what, you will always be magical!"

Luisa and Dinah are wearing the Touchstone bracelet they bought the day Dinah's little idea was born.

About the Illustrator

Angie Alape was born and raised in Colombia. She grew up drawing on all the cardboard boxes around her to create magical worlds in which to play with her siblings. As she was studying graphic design, a Chilean publishing house asked her to illustrate some Colombian folk tales for a picture book on which they were working. She decided to try it, and has been working as a freelance illustrator ever since. Her work has been published in digital and print media in Colombia, Peru, France, England, and the United States. Her clients include Hachette, HP, OUP, Beaming Books, Auzou, Ediciones Norma, Ediciones Pichoncito, Moonbug, Insert Coin Animation Studios, and more. In her free time, she can be found playing with her adopted dogs and looking for places to enjoy a good meal during the weekend.

About the Book Designer

Michelle Radomski is a self-taught designer, mandala artist, and champion for the Art of Brave collection. From the moment she opened her first box of sixty-four crayons, Michelle knew she was born to create. She has been a graphic designer and book designer for more than forty years, and has completed nearly 10,000 creative projects for corporations, nonprofits, entrepreneurs, publishers, and independent authors. Over a decade ago, she was inspired to create mandalas using the letters of empowering words. These unique expressions of energy have been sold around the world.

Michelle is currently birthing a body of work she calls The Create Brave Experience—a space in which creative humans of all types and experience levels gather in community to make and share the art that lives in their hearts. She designs and publishes a quarterly magazine to showcase the creative expressions of the artists in the Create Brave community.

Printed in the USA
CPSIA information can be obtained
at www.ICGtesting.com
CBHW041924031123
1672CB00001B/1